First published in the United Kingdom in 2002
by Charmed Hole Publications, Poolewe,
Ross-shire IV22 2JZ Scotland

ISBN 0 9522707 0 6

A CIP catalogue record for this book is
available from the British Library

www. atisha.org.uk
Printed and bound by
Polestar Aberdeen Limited
Made in Scotland

for Mohiza,

PEACE ROOTS

Poems
&
Aphorisms

by
Atisha McGregor Auld

With Best Wishes for 2003

Atisha McGregor Auld

Published by

CHARMED | HOLE
PUBLICA | IONS

With special thanks to:-

Edited by Kenneth Urquhart
Typeset by Barry Richardson
Translations:
Gaelic by Roy G. Wentworth
Latin by Mairi Miller
Illustrations:
Author photographed by Judith South
Cover image edited by Jim Buchanan
"Baosbheinn" (Front Cover) by Peter R. Barton
"Deer" by Terry Barron Kirkwood
Acknowledgement:
Quotation by Ted Hughes on rear cover
reproduced by kind permission of his Estate

Book designed by Helen Meek

The Roots of Peace
may be found in Nature

CONTENTS

Key to footnotes
Where there is a Gaelic version it is denoted by a **G**
Where there is a Latin translation it is denoted by an **L**
Additional and Further notes are to be found
at the end of the book and these are denoted
on the relevant page by an **N**

A Gaelic Prayer

My soul goes into the mountains,
Deep to where peace may be found:
Take my soul Oh God
And change it into the wind
And with your breath
Allow me to breathe
Purity, Wisdom and Freedom
Over the lands you survey.

Amen

Ùrnaigh

Tha m' anam a' dol a chum nam beann,
Domhainn far am faighear sìth:
Gabh ri m' anam a Dhé
Agus dèan 'atharrachadh 'na ghaoith
Agus le t' anail
Leig le m' anail-sa bhith séideadh
Glaine, Gliocas is Saorsa
Thar nan tìr a tha 'nad choimhead.

Amen

A Meditation

Love all
Take nothing
Give everything.

A Valentine

Hearts touch
Bodies close
Spirits soar –
Wish that you were mine.

Age

Life dies –
Youth fades
Days done.
Autumn leaves
Dead grass
Setting sun.
Energy spent
Thoughts lost
Time gone.
Here now
There soon:
Move on.
Heaven reached
Friends found
End begun.
Souls met
Happiness yet
Earth forget –
Aye and Anon.

Androgynous

Which way to dress?
Left, right,
Cross dress?
Aided by
This one, that one
Cover up
Come out
Tied
By convention,
Genes, jeans
Attract
Attention,
Waiting
For the right time
To express
Experience
Life.

Anniversary

I

We met today
A year ago
Je t'aime, je t'aime
I love you so.

II

We met today
Two years ago
Oyez, oyez
I love you so.

III

Today we met
Three years ago
So sad, so sad
You left me so.

Another Valentine

To care and to share
All year
Is all I want to do
With you
So please let me be
A part
Of your heart
And I will love you
If you will love me too?

Apart

Apart –
Not for long
I hope

Thoughts
In your mind
I hope

Missing
Me the while
I hope

Tears
Away for now
I hope

Feelings
Back again
I hope

Together
Sometime soon
I hope

Love –
For tomorrow
I hope.

Auld Reekie

Edinburgh's castle
Chapels and Mound
With its holy pools
Of Dunsapie,
Duddingston
And St. Margaret
Where swans white
And feathered
Protect the saints'
Hallowed ground;
Where stones
Of St Anthony
Below Arthur's Seat
Survey the path
Where pilgrims
Used to walk
Their way
To and from
Incholm grand –
The site of many
A religious
Ceremony performed.
We all await
The day when
Your streets
Now paved
With tourism,
Commerce and industry
Make way for
Something better

With which to
Fill man's mind.
The Holy-Rood
Lies in wait
For your
Honoured time –
So await we.

Auld Scotia

Glasgow's streets mean and wide
The big issue lies here –
Marxism, fascism,
Anarchy, monarchy,
Homelessness, poverty.
Where are we going
As a nation proud?
A nation who once
The army did fill;
A nation once from
Whom countries were bred
And brains did emigrate
To places afar.
Why are we seeking
To destroy ourselves
When we were once great
And still are?

Being

Nothing matters anymore.
We are all matter
Blown by the atoms
We are all part of
Into a lifeless sea,
A sea of limitless life
For those who wish to live on.

Being Alone

Thank you for coming into my life,
For every hour that you loved me,
For the bond that caused us both
To share in so much happiness,
And most of all for the chance
To learn to grow in love.
Your heart leaves me now
Only to linger on ...

Caribbee

De white man teach us
De ways of de world
Oh Lordy, Lordy
From tribal life hurled

Black skin, white skin
Coloured, mulatto
Oh Lordy, Lordy
Life jubilato

De bananas green
De bananas ripe
Oh Lordy, Lordy
Away our tears wipe

We make de ginger
We juice de limes
Oh Lordy, Lordy
Dis be bad times

We shall be free
De old people say
Oh Lordy, Lordy
When be dat day

De chilren play
In de chattels wid laughter
Oh Lordy, Lordy
Protect dem after

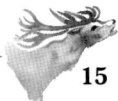

We plant de yam
We sow de cucumber
Oh Lordy, Lordy
We be no humbler

We pick de cotton
We cut de cane
Oh Lordy, Lordy
Again and again

We catch de fish
De sheep we slaughter
Oh Lordy, Lordy
We live as we oughta

De cows dey sit
Wid egrets by
Oh Lordy, Lordy
Our time is nigh

De ships of wood
De men of iron
Oh Lordy, Lordy
Spare us de hurricane

De palm trees sway
De mahogany grow
Oh Lordy, Lordy
De stars dey glow

De moon lie flat
De sun is strong
Oh Lordy, Lordy
Keep us young

De rum we drink
De punch is sure
Oh Lordy, Lordy
For now and evermore

We eat de bread-fruit
We take de coconut water
Oh Lordy, Lordy
From now til de hereafter

In church we sing
De tambourines ring
Oh Lordy, Lordy, Lordy
Praise de good Lord.

Childbirth

My soul goes into my womb,
Deep to where life may be found:
Take my pain Oh God
And turn it into a child,
And may this child
With your blessing
Be joyful, strong and wise.

Clouds

Clouds up on high
Floating
Shifting
Changing
Shielding the face of the sun

Clouds gathered together
Graceful
Useful
Purposeful
Chatting to the purple sky

Clouds blown by the wind
Rushing
Moving
Hurrying
Bringing rain to the earth

Clouds breaking up
Tearful
Joyful
Meaningful
Leaving a pathway to heaven.

Crofters' Song *or Autumn*

Air chill
Geese fly
Stags roar
Autumn now

Lambs grown
Calves weaned
Hay in
Peat stacked

Stars bright
Days short
Fires lit
God thanked.

Duanag a' Chroiteir *neo Am Foghar*

Daimh a' bùirich
Foghar a-nis
Thig fuachd; tuitidh
'N duilleag chlis

Uan na othaisg
Laogh na ghamhainn
Mòine sa chruaich
Feur san iodhlainn

Rionnagan, teine
Là geàrr, odhar
Taing don Tì
Thug dhuinn am foghar.

Cupid's Wings

I still wait
To hear
Cupid's wings
Beating softly,
Awakening
My heart,
And to hear
That you await
Once again
Love's tender
Ritual.

Death

Death catches us all in the end,
Like the cold that eludes us all winter
And finally envelops us in the spring.
The summer sun warms the heart
That feels but not the one that
Does not beat. Beaten by life,
The heart ultimately dies, taking
The life within without to another sphere –
A plane to which we will all sometime fly
Only to meet again with the same souls,
The same lessons, until our sins
Are worn away by wearisome repetition,
Only to leave a purified spirit
In charge of its own destiny – to fly
Hither and thither amongst the stars
And to find its resting place once again.

Early Summer

Buttercups, bluebells and daisies
I saw in the fields to-day
And heard the chaffinch,
Blackbird and thrush
Singing their hearts away.

The deer came down from the hills
Some greener grass to find,
But the hinds hung back
Their calves to protect
And sought to avoid mankind.

A mare stood heavily in foal,
Whilst all the lambs their
Mothers needed less,
And each and everything
The nature spirits did bless.

Earth Energy

Sacred grove
Druid oaks
Time foretold

Whispering leaves
Stones sure
Alignment bold

Lunar rays
Ephemeral growth
Life cajoled

Planetary forms
Celestial gaze
Days unfold

Mystic haunts
Magic spell
As of old

Earth sings
Vibrations change
Man humbled.

Easter

Easter
is the time
for rolling eggs
and counting frogs
and remembering all
those past and
present who
have died to
save the
World

Equinoctial Gales

Angry wind
Trees sway
Clouds gather
Destruct, decay

Leaves blown
Up, around
Quickly fall
To the ground

Heavy rain
Flattened grass
Soaked, drenched
Storm will pass

Trunks upright
Branches down
Split, broken
All is blown

Over now
Newness sensed
Peace, still
Earth is cleansed.

For Beyond

Oh come with me
Flower of Loveliness
Let us show the world
What it is to be

What it is to be
In a future world
That exists in happiness
With thee and me

All shall see
The world in peace
And loveliness beholden
For now and ever be.

Forever

Forever be together,
Enjoy, share,
Treasure, care –
Love as one
Touch happiness
Laugh freely
Be true
Love simply
Feel deeply
So gently
Completely
Be happy
Together forever.

Full Circle

Cycles wheel
Noiselessly
In and out
Of traffic lined
Head to tail,
Nose to fumes,
Lead filled
Heavy hearts
At nature's dismay.

Glen Luss

Ancient bridge
Sheep's head
Rough stone

Snow falls
Ram stands
There alone

Farm sits
Windy ridge
Trees blown

Fire burns
Sparks fly
Timbers groan

Burn runs
Animals tread
Paths unknown

Stars rise
Lovers walk
Time bemoan.

Great Langdale

Oh Langdale!
Your pikes, force
And mountains grand
Peaked with snow
And the site
Of parliament old
Where sheep now graze
And yew trees rest
Your peace is
Unsurpassable
When touched by
Those who walk
Your old track ways,
Once by coffins
And pack horse trod.
Drovers too your
Way did go,
Making a stop
At old Chapel Stile –
Your chapel in the
Rocks where all
Did pray.
Peaks, pikes,
Fells and force
Show us
The way.

Hallowe'en

Feathers are feathers
Toads are toads
Feathers from pigeons
Feathers from crows

Fire and frost
Eagle's claw
Raven's beak
Sheep's jaw

Feathers are feathers
Toads are toads
Feathers from pigeons
Feathers from crows

Cauldron hot
Hare's foot
Birch bark
Black soot

Feathers are feathers
Toads are toads
Feathers from pigeons
Feathers from crows

Dead leaves
Dark dells
Cats howl
Quaint spells

Feathers are feathers
Toads are toads
Feathers from pigeons
Feathers from crows

Corn ripe
Cock's comb
Magic wells
Witches roam

Feathers are feathers
Toads are toads
Feathers from pigeons
Feathers from crows

Foxes teeth
Owl's wing
Ills cured
Spirits sing

Feathers are feathers
Toads are toads
Feathers from pigeons
Feathers from crows.

Hardraw Scar

A rainbow appears
And disappears
As if by magic,
Playing hide and seek
With the sun,
Coating the spray
With many colours.
The bandstand empty
Makes music no more
But listens to the
Thunderous roar
Of Hardraw's Force.
One hundred feet
It drops below
A pine standing proudly
Above the fall –
Only the oak looks
On in dismay for
Soon the time will come
When it will plunge
Into cold waters
Of the Scar – the waters
That have travelled
From Lovely Seat
And Stags Fell nearby.
The rocks mostly unmoved,
Save those behind the force
Where man can no longer tread,
Provide nature's backdrop
To one of England's
Highest waterfalls.

Sandstone, iron ore,
Limestone and shale
Fragmented – guard
The Dragon Force
By day and night.

Hope

Time came
Time went.
Both loved,
Love spent.

Feelings raw
Hurt pride;
Longings yet
Deep inside.

Mine still
Memories fond,
Hope lingers
For beyond.

Human Love

The stars await
The shining hour
When sun and moon
Doth send their power –
Let human minds
The wisdom know
Of heavenly secrets
Far below.

When humans let
Their emotions go
Then 'tis the time
To reap and sow,
To gather all
The knowledge in
And protect all souls
From mortal sin.

Leap Year

Mind confused
Thoughts jumbled
Painful heart
Times remembered.
To love you truly
Was my intent
But solitude and time
Now seem more important.
Please wait until
I can feel again
And then I will
Give you everything –
Everything you want
For greater happiness.
Pray to God that never
Will I inflict on you
Any pain – only a love
So tender and gentle
That makes you complete
From yourself within.

Let Glasgow Flourish

The Kelvin flows
on through time.
A tyre sits
on a flat stone
where ducks
used to live;
branches
weighed down
with heaviness
rest in water
drinking in the
effluent.
Supermarket trolleys
on permanent vacation
lie basking
in the sun.
Plastic bags
pink and blue
white and striped
monitor the wind's
mood for the day.
A tree stands dead
after eight years
of growth – unable
to stand the pressure
of life any more.
Older, stronger trees
remain steadfast
withstanding all
attempts to hasten
their demise.

Cans, bottles and
coloured wrappers
exhibit themselves
like pieces of
modern sculpture
brightening the day
of passers-by.
Dogs sniff and
sniff again
whilst performing
their daily ritual.
Blackberries wait
in the shade
hoping to ripen
and be of use
to man and bird
before the winter
toil begins.
Only the sweet
smell of limes
rises above the
stench of the river,
once a natural haven
for homeless wildlife.
Now all that has
passed away.
Man and nature strive
to live and breathe
in amongst the
polluted eons.
Let Nature Flourish.

Life

Rocks grow out of trees
Trees grow out of rocks
Trees grow out of trees
The Rowan from the Oak
The Holly from the Chestnut
The Birch from the Willow.
We cannot depend on
Ourselves for growth
All life is sustained
By another.

May Day

All earthly vows
Are set aside
When morning dew
Kisses garlands
Of flowers
Wrapped around
The maypole fair,
Where youth
Their souls
Do gladly bare
And celebrate
The ancient
Feast-day
Of Beltane –
And summer too
When the gay
Festivities
Old and new
Are heralded
By the bold
Cuckoo
So that the
Merrymaking
May now begin ...

Mid-Summer *or Summer Solstice*

High sun
Bare grass,
Passions rise
Dreams pass.

Shadows long
Solstice here;
Candles burn
Softly there.

Night short
Love done –
Breezes cool
Warmth gone.

Mòr-Rìgh *or Maree*

Sheep masquerading as monks
On the mound
Rath-thìodhlaicidh
Maybe
Maelrubha, Columba
And many more
Lie waiting on
Isle Maree.

Mòr-Rìgh,
Great King,
With knowledge for all
Your Pictish stone
Lies somnambulently
In Lòn Dubh.

Moon's phases
Pagan feasts
Focused on a god
One for all
Now to return
This time
Coming
The next millennium.

Mother's Day and the Vernal Equinox – Sunday 21st March

Mother's Day
Mother Earth
Both share
In giving birth
On this bounteous
Day of the Vernal
Equinox – equal
In sharing
Nature's joys
And in producing
For one another's
Survival – let (Wo)
Man rejoice.

Mountain Peaks

Stones, steps,
Crags grey
Steep heights

Feet touch
Ancient core
Way to Heaven

Feet in Hell
Heart aspires
Jagged peaks

Air pure
Spirits dwell
Ridges high

Soul uplifted
Spirit soars
Healing done

Whole, complete,
Strong again
Descent begun.

Night

Waters calm
Trees reflect
Moon's gaze

Toil done
Setting sun
Sky ablaze

Wind still
Owl hoots
Sheep graze

Dark follows
Peace falls
Night always

Shafts of light
Birds awake
Morning haze.

On Departing for Ireland

You dreamt I left you
With no farewell
No kiss
I too was dreaming
You were crying
Sad
I comforted you.

I am leaving for a
Short while
Soon
But we shall say goodbye
Kiss
And I will take your love
With me.

Opera Viva

The stage bare
Crowded with
Memories
Arias performed
As never before.
Oh heavenly
Notes
Transport my soul
Seduce me
Till the curtain
Drops.
Quest'anima è oppressa

Passions aroused
Intrigue
Enchantment
Stimulation
Deprivation
Dénouements
Overtures
Instrumental
In introducing
Scenes of love
Hate, violence
Couched in sets
Of fine array.

N

Costumes bright
Costumes drab
Props bizarre
Leading to escapism
For all to enjoy.
Oh heavenly
Voices
Uplift my soul
Seduce me
Till the curtain
Drops.
Quest'anima è oppressa

Out of Ancient Manuscripts
or Ex Libris

Deo Gratis et
Cantate Domino
Canticum Novum
Psalms Medieval
Voices pure
Missals, chant
Sepia script
Monastic sound

Figures kneeling
Prayers upheld
Wingèd souls
Light beheld
Sun, stars
Realms on high
Dragon fire
Apocalypse nigh

Heraldic verse
Rose hue
Floral tributes
Peacock blue
Gilt edged
Parchment faded
Ancient reamed
Leather bound

Infant son
Mother true
Heaven sent
Devoted hand
God augment
Chosen land
Byzantium
And Europe too.

Passing Away

Birds fly
Bird eats fly
Cat eats bird
Cat eats fish
I eat fish
We all die
Sometime, somehow.

The wind that
Carries my soul
Away brings
The fly.

Royal Tunbridge Wells

Tunbridge Wells,
Royal by decree,
Since George's time
In the early
Eighteenth century.
Queen Victoria
On a donkey
Rode to frequent
Your healing ways –
With well and rocks
And water pure
Enough to win
A Spa's acclaim.
The Pump Room
And the Pantiles too
Heritage did add
Where music played
With grace and charm.
No longer now
A Spa of fame
But more so
A commuter paradise
Where most folk
Come and go
To gain wealth
And not health.

St. Kilda (Hirta) – 1930s

Atlantic waves
Sea alive
Gulls cry
Shags dive

Men climb
Stacks grand
Strength prove
Back on land

Sheep horned
Gannet's oil
Lamps primed
End of toil

Boat secure
Sail mended
Compass set
Course intended

Ocean vast
Lines taut
Men stare
Fish caught

Women work
Bairns die
Religion strong
End nigh

Folk distraught
Island left
No return
All bereft.

Sculpture of Horse and Man
or Energy Exchange

Knees held
Head resting
Meditative pose

Horse holding
Man's frame
Souls in repose

Legs straight
Tail erect
Pressed nose

Abdomen round
Bodies still
Spirits loose

Foal unborn
Life contemplate
Foetus grows

Energies restored
Parting soon
Both propose.

Seashore

Waves land on the shore
Sea shifts sand
Sand sifts shells
Shells lie entwined
Seaweed lies lifeless
Life inside
Washed, cleansed
By the turning tide –
Mother-of-pearl, coral
Riches from the ocean
All lie here
Basking in the sun.

Sinning

Love
Lust
Desire
Infatuation

Touch
Feel
Have
Self-gratification

Flesh
Longing
Pleasure
Fornication

Seduce
Take
Hold
Mortification

Abstain
Celibate
Pure
Divination.

Spring Lambs – *An Invocation*

Little lambs
Born this day
God protect you
Where'er you stray.

Lambs so white
With faces black
Eat the grass
Till logs we stack.

Amen

Springtime

Waters flow
Mountain tops
Covered in snow.
Snow white doves
Hatching soon
Under the Worm Moon.
Yellow flowers
Daffodil, Forsythia,
Cowslip and Mahonia
All do bloom.
Grass green
All the while
Doth grow
Before the lambs
Do show.
Earth sings on high,
Beneath, below
"All awake
And enjoy until
The leaves fall again.
Amen".

Supplication

Thine be the glory
The moon and stars your provenance
I worship you daily
When I take bread
Even when there is an eclipse
And the day becomes darkened
O Supreme One
I am thine.

Supplicatio

Tibi gloria sit
E luna stellisque ortus es
In dies te venero
Ubi panem edo
Et, sole luna occluso,
Dies nox fixit.
O Supreme,
Tu es dominus meus.

Swans

I dreamt
We were flying high
Beside the low peaks
Covered in snow –

We were both
Swans
Beautiful and strong.

You tried to move out
From the shelter
Of the hill,
But I bade you
Draw back
For there was turbulence
Without.

The day was clear
And bright
And we were both cleansed.

The Dove

To me you came
As a dove
White, mottled
With feathers grey,
Wild, now tame –
For me to love.

You came to me
With an air
Of charm –
Here, settled
Away from harm –
For me to love.

The Mind

The mind
Flips, turns
Churns
Until peace can be found
The peace for which it yearns
Until it reaches heaven.
Heaven on earth
Or heaven above
It matters not which.

The Oak Tree
or Womb Man's Thoughts

An Oak
I Ask
The Past.
The Oak
Spoke:
Try, spy
Man.
Uni-form,
Flesh torn.
Oak tree
See
No man,
Only Wo-man.

The Parting

You left
We parted
So sad
You drove
Me mad
We'd been
Together
And I'd hoped
Forever
To fulfil
All my dreams.

But time cut us short
And I know that I ought

To get on with my life
Without dreaming anymore
Of good times in store
And save Mother Earth
From inevitable death
For now and evermore.

Life may be cut short
Who cares? I know I ought.

The River

You are to me as a river
  Flowing,
    Ebbing,
  Gently flowing,
    Babbling,
      Singing, bursting,
        Twisting,
      Turning,
        Winding,
          Yielding,
      Flowing,
    Merrily meandering
  On your way –
You are to me as a river.

An Abhainn

Tha thu leamsa mar abhainn
  A' lìonadh,
   A' tràghadh,
  Gu socair a' sruthadh,
   A' dol sa phlubadaich,
    A' tighinn le òran is le maoim,
    A' cuagalais,
   A' lùbadh,
    Ag iadhadh,
     A' gèilleadh,
    A' sruthadh,
   Gu subhach a' cur nan caran
  Air do shlighe –
Tha thu leamsa mar abhainn.

The Stag

Heraldic horns
Resting high
Nobly pointing
To the sky

Points twelve,
Fourteen or more
Guaranteeing
A royal score.

The Willow, the Reed and the Elder

Your being,
as supple as the
tree of your birth,
the Willow,
winsome
and
slender,
seeks knowledge
under the lunar
influence
and in so doing
touches mine
searching for
truth and balance
through the bitterness
of the Reed
and the sweetness
of the Elder.
When time
has revealed
all things true,
then may our
entwining flourish
and blossom –
one bending with
the other
through unending storms
and days of delight.
Peace will reign
in the forest.

To a Dovecote – *A Blessing*

By waters deep
And trees high
Leaves on branches
So you fly.

Peace be with you
As you rest
Raised up there
In your nest.

Winds blow strong
Rain fall light
The gods protect you
Through each night.

Amen

To a Gravestone

For whom do you mourn oh stone?
Whose body lies beneath your head?
Time has eroded their name and
Obliterated it into nothingness.
What is in a name anyway?
Few of us are given names
With which at birth we can recall
The spirit by which we were known
In former lives.
Help us to search oh stone
Within ourselves for that name
Which links us to our past
And by which we may be
Recognised in the present.
Mine is *Atisha*
What is yours?

To a Healer Friend

Thank you for everything –
For friendship given,
Understanding my ways,
My thoughts and ideas.
No judgement given,
Only healing and help,
Prayers offered up for all
From you – so close to God.
You, who can tell the mind's
Most innermost thoughts
Oh that you would do for yourself
That which you do for others!
Thank you for everything.

To a Horse's Head
Carved Out of Marble

Chiselled head
Marbled veins
Sicilian stone

Mouth flanged
Ancient eyes
Stare alone

Ears flat
Smooth neck
Erogenous zone

Chinese art
Medieval horse
Life condone

Nostrils flared
Looks proud
Rare stallion.

Trees

How pretty the trees,
they stand proudly
on the hill,
a mere skeleton
of themselves
waiting for the
sap to reach
their outermost parts
when black shall
become green
and birds shall seek
out their nests
or make anew
for eggs fertile
will soon wing their way
to sites secluded,
then the cycle
of nature will
begin again
how pretty the trees so handsomely clad...

True Love

To take you to Paradise
I gently wish I could
And there you would
Sleep away your fears,
Dry your tears,
And I would guard you
Whilst you dreamt
Of all it is
You desire –
And when you awoke
I would be there
To caress you
Or fade away
Whichever you prefer.

Vibrations of Nature

The shapes of the clouds
The patterns in the sky
The song of the rain
The voices in the wind
The size of the snowflake
The ripples in the sand
All come and go with the sun,
The moon, the planets and the stars.

Wasdale Head

Your gentle rain
Washes my fair skin;
Soft gentle rain,
Pure and cleansing.
My heart feels
The joy of its
Natural purity
Sent from heaven
As a gift from
The gods.

Your graveyard sits
Surrounded by yews
Where bones lie
Nourishing your growth.
My spirit touches
The grandeur
Of the peaks nearby
On reading the
Epitaphs that rest here
In peace.

Your ancient inn
With warmth to
Revive the soul
Welcomes all alike;
Food and drink
Await us here.
Let us remember
To thank the unseen hand
That makes all things possible.

White Lilies

I dreamt
Last night
That a lily
Stood by my bed
White petalled
And scented
With memories
From the past.

I leant forward
To touch
The stamens
When six petals
Fell about me
And caressed me
Back to sleep.

Were you that
Lilium Album
Invoking me
To reach out
And touch
Your soul?

I pray 'tis so
For dreams
Are made of this.

Wild Flowers

Flag Iris –
Yellow hue,
Green dye
Colours true?

Orchid bright
Hiding there
Out of sight,
Species rare.

Purple strong
Heather bells.
Summer's here
Nature tells.

Dog Rose,
Dainty flowers
Musk scent
Healing powers.

Foxgloves many
Fingers pointed;
Healthy heart
So anointed.

Thistles high –
Prickly stems:
Emblematic
Diadems.

Flowers wild
Unpicked there;
We thank thee
With reverent air.

Winter in Haddington

Gnarled roots
Frozen ground
Sun stares
Empty sky
Winter haze
Birds fly
Trees sleep
Leaves drop
Frosted bridge
River swims
Silent all
Nature dreams
Dogs bark
Hungry howl
Broken plaque
Royal tree
Bells ring
Graves cold
Children sing
Christmas nigh.

ADDITIONAL NOTES

1   A Gaelic Prayer
Inspired by Baosbheinn, 875m, Wester Ross.

2   Ùrnaigh
Le smuaintean air Badhaisbheinn, 2,986 troigh, Ros an Iar.

10   Auld Reekie
Old name for Edinburgh.

12   Auld Scotia
Written in Glasgow.

15   Caribbee
Written on a visit to Barbados.
(See further note on page 88)

25   Earth Energy
Inspired by the terrain at Kernsary, Wester Ross.

31   Glen Luss
Written near Loch Lomond, Dunbarton-shire.

32   Great Langdale
Written in the Lake District.

35   Hardraw Scar
Written in the Yorkshire Dales.

45   Mòr-Rìgh or Maree
Inspired by the surrounding areas of Isle Maree, Wester Ross. Rath-thìodhlaicidh – Gaelic for Lair or Grave-plot.

47   Mountain Peaks
Inspired on the Bealach nam Bó, Applecross, Wester Ross.

50   Opera Viva
Quest'anima è oppressa
"My soul is overwhelmed"
Maria Stuarda by Donizetti (Act II).

FURTHER NOTES

The poem CARIBBEE portrays the sense of rhythm
found in the Caribbean island of Barbados. It also
expresses the Islanders' way of life with its hardships
and blessings whilst emphasising their faith in God.

Their life today, as much before, is still lived close to
nature but with a western influence always at their back.
May they find their own way in the world in the new
millennium with steadfastness.

If a refrain is required, use the verse:
"We pick de cotton
We cut de cane" etc.

The lines in SUPPLICATION are dedicated to the Irish saint Columba (c. 521-597) whose death was commemorated at the end of the 20th century.
It has been translated into Latin, it being the language of early Christian worship rather than Gaelic.

This earnest prayer has been composed with both the names of the natural notes of the tonic sol-fa scale and the Lord's Prayer in mind. The words in the Gaelic are identical in pronunciation with the above sol-fa scale nomenclature. Each Gaelic word has a meaning which has been translated into English (*emphasised here in bold italics*) and incorporated into this supplication.

In medieval Gaelic verse, a poem would often begin and end with the same word. This was called 'dùnadh'.

♩   **Gaelic**

Doh	*Thine* be the glory	*Do*
Ray	The *moon* and stars your provenance	*Ré*
Me	*I* worship you daily	*Mi*
Fah	When I take *bread*	*Fàbh*
Soh	Even when there is an *eclipse*	*Soadh*
Lah	And the *day* becomes darkened	*Là*
Te	O Supreme *One*	*Tì*
Doh	I am *thine*	*Do*

SEE GAELIC-ENGLISH DICTIONARY
COMPILED BY EDWARD DWELLY